MW00426736

Five YEARS IN THE MAKING

I grew up in Santa Monica- skating and surfing. March 1999: I picked up a copy of Spin Magazine: an article called the "Lords of Dogtown" really HIT A NERVE. I knew it would be a cool movie I was working for Fox as a producer and I bought the story rights from author, Greg Beato. My father and fellow producer, Art Linson, also really believed in the story. (Besides The "Untouchables", "Heat", and 20 other films, Art had produced another classic teen film, "Fast Times at Ridgemont High.")

Through mutual friends, I hooked up with Jay Adams and I got his life rights. Next, Skip Engblom and Craig Stecyk signed on.

Producer-John Linson

For me it was just a scam- I figured...sure, take this up front cash- one movie pitch in 10,000 gets to the popcorn zone... Skip Engblom

I didn't trust John Linson at first, no way. When I found out about his dad, Art Linson, the credibility was there.-Tony Alva

Next, I needed Tony Alva's life rights. He and I met at a party, but things were so tense we almost brawled on the balcony. After he left, I learned he had pinched my girlfriend's ass.

Producer-John Linson

4

When Hollywood got to the story before any of us did – it really knocked me out. I decided to tell **the real story before somebody else screwed it up**, so in March 2000, I started making the documentary. I wouldn't sign over my life rights to the feature unless I was involved in writing the script. So the Linsons and I started discussing this possibility. In the meantime, I finished the doc and sent a rough cut to Sundance in October of 2000.   Stacy Peralta

DOGTOWN AND Z-BOYZ" takes Park City by storm
Stacy wins Best Documentry Director at the Sundance Film Festival 2001

After the success of the doc, I got hired to write the script. I went to Alva, Engblom, Stecyk and Adams and got their support and stories. While I was writing, I changed my character's name to Jamie Perez as it was too much of a distraction to use my real name. I probably wrote close to twenty drafts of the script, developing it and re-developing it with the producers who had a very strong hand in helping to shape the eventual story that emerged.

The Dogtown experience lasted roughly seven years, from 1973, when we were young teens, up through the birth of the urethane wheel and the rise of backyard pool skating, then ending with our professional careers in 1980. To fit into a three-act dramatic structure, we condensed time into roughly three years with many of our random and disconnected experiences combined and re-shaped. **-Stacy Peralta**

l of the Z-Boyz went into the process knowing that our
periences would be compressed
d puzzled together in a form that
y not be exactly factual, but would in
t capture

Laemmle
Monica 4 Plex

Q: Was Catherine Hardwicke your first choice to direct this film?

Absolutely, she was our first choice...after Sean Penn, Fred Durst, David Fincher.

I met Stacy in an acting class in the 80's — I was intrigued when he recited a monologue while slapping stickers on a skateboard. He introduced me to Craig Stecyk and invited me to premieres of "Bones Brigades" videos. We both worked on Thrashin' → I was the Production Designer, Stacy was 2ND UNIT Director, and Tony Alva played a "DAGGER" — CAT HARDWICKE

David Fincher started casting and location scouting, but by mid 2003, he and Sony parted company. Shortly thereafter, I saw Catherine's movie "thirteen." Her film blew me away, to say the least. I immediately called John Linson and told him that she was "the" director. He shot me down with "I've heard her film is a Saturday afternoon special." STACY

TWO MONTHS LAPSED BEFORE I FINALLY DECIDED TO WATCH 'THIRTEEN.' AFTER THE FIRST TWO MINUTES, I KNEW SHE WAS THE PERFECT DIRECTOR FOR LORDS OF DOGTOWN — JOHN LINSON

When I got hired, I raced down to Oceanside and hung out with Tony Alva and his sister Kathy, looking thru scrapbooks & listening to great stories about the scrappy kids from the "wrong side of the tracks." Kathy said "It was harder for us to dream." I loved her spirit & humor & wrote her into the film.

6

we

NEXt STOP: HAWAII. My first morning, I watched Jay surf 14 foot waves at Pipeline, then was instructed to drive the rental car to an empty pool, climb a ladder, and "liberate" mangos from a neighbor's tree. 20 minutes later, JAY smashed a ripe mango on my back — HARRD — then spooked an 85 yr old granny at a restaurant. I didn't stop taking notes for 3 days. –CAT

I think it is an honor to have somebody interested in what we did. It's cool. You usually have to die before people do that kind of stuff.

JAY ADAMS

For five years I was on cruise control. Next thing you know I'm taking meetings, the camera's rolling and the road show started - Skip Engblom

I have a lot of respect for John Linson now, he persevered – the film basically got done on his terms.
Tony Alva

Little John is like a rabid pit bull.

Guess that's what it takes. SKIP ENGBLOM

JAY ADAMS

You really never know what's going to happen next when you hang with JAY. Its a Fucking RUSH

— Emile

EMILE HIRSCH
AS

EMILE HIRSCH, JAY ADAMS, TONY ALVA, REBECCA DE MORNAY

Gosh, I sure do miss, playing JAY Adams.
It was more fun than being me! — Emile

WHEN GOD CREATED THE ARCHETYPICAL CALIFORNIA KID,
THE ORIGINAL VIRUS, HE SAID
—LET THERE BE JAY ADAMS—

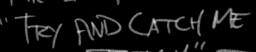

THE IMP SEZ:
"TRY AND CATCH ME
BITCH"

For my 19th birthday I went and visited Jay and I'll never forget that Hawaii trip. He told me some things I don't think he's told very many people, which was really helpful.

Jay's friends call him one radical little Rat.
— Emile

EMILE WALKED INTO MY OFFICE, CARPET-OLLIED ON A BOARD, THEN SAID "I'M GONNA BE JAY ADAMS," I NEVER AUDITIONED ANY BODY ELSE.
— CAT

Emile showed me what it's like to be a serious actor and a teenager at the same time. We would do everything, from making fun of people on & off set to getting into deep & serious conversations about life & Marlon Brando. He is the ish.
— Mike

MICHAEL ANGARANO AKA SID

How humiliating, some one putting MAKE UP on me for a magazine shoot. I really dislike wearing make up. Guys with make up on look what they are... guys with make up on. Next...

11

Any bad thing I did I blamed on Tony.
VIC

Alva girlz rule!!

VICTOR RASUK
AS
TONY ALVA

It didn't get better than this. The guy was so cool about me portraying him. And it showed so much in our personal life. *VIC*

13

I worked with Victor
one on one daily and
it shows in his attitude.
I wanted him to be
pro on and off the
board. His intensity
& competitive spirit
was very evident from
day one.
love, T. Alva

14

TONY WASN'T
JUST A ROCK STAR—

he was a deeply charismatic person whose entire identity was skateboarding. It was rare to see him have a bad day skating. —Stacy

WHEN VICTOR GOT OFF THE PLANE— HE WAS TOTAL NEW YORK— HIP HOP STYLE — BAGGY PANTS, NIKE AIRS — ALL "YO YO YO." I'M LIKE "NO NO NO!" NOBODY at sony can see you like this— you've got 2 days to lose that shit and go WEST COAST. Tony got him Vans and a board and he wasn't allowed to go back home for 5 months. —CAT

JOHN ROBINSON
AS
STACY PERALTA

I wasn't until 2 weeks into training that I got to meet Stacy. He had been so swamped finishing Riding Giants that he could only meet at 10:00 pm. "Bicknell at 10:00." I skated down the boardwalk from my apartment on Rose and as I got closer I could just make out a figure flying down the hill under the street lights. After that Night I got Stacy. He showed me how to Saturn using my toe on the tail of the board. We told stories and he gave me the history of the Ocean and Bicknell. The guy really glows when he skates!

JCR

JOHN AND I MET SEVERAL WEEKS BEFORE PRODUCTION WAS SET TO BEGIN. IT WAS NIGHT-TIME, EARLY SUMMER 2004. WE HAD SPOKEN BY PHONE AND AGREED TO MEET AT BICKNELL HILL WITH OUR SKATEBOARDS. I ARRIVED EARLY AND BEGAN SKATING THE HILL, WHICH IS THE SAME HILL ALL OF US ON THE ORIGINAL ZEPHYR TEAM USED TO SKATE BACK IN THE 70'S, DOING BERTS ETC.
AFTER ABOUT 30 MINUTES OF SKATING I LOOKED DOWN THE BOARDWALK AND SAW THIS KID IN HIS LATE TEENS SKATING TOWARD ME. HE HAD VERY LONG BLONDE HAIR, HE WAS WEARING OLD SCHOOL STRAIGHT-LEG CORDS, A 70'S STYLE TEE-SHIRT, VANS OLD SCHOOL BLUE DECK SHOES AND HE WAS RIDING A HOMEMADE WOODEN BOARD THAT WAS ABOUT 5 INCHES WIDE WITH TINY ORIGINAL ISSUE URETHANE WHEELS. SEEING THE IMAGE WAS LIKE LOOKING BACK THROUGH A TIME MACHINE.
I WAS RELIEVED TO SEE THAT JOHN COULD SKATE. HE WASN'T STIFF OR AWKWARD BUT IN FACT HAD A VERY NATURAL STYLE. BUT THE THING ABOUT HIM THAT REALLY GOT MY INTEREST WAS HOW MUCH DESIRE HE HAD TO GET IT RIGHT. HE WAS DEAD-SET DETERMINED FROM THE START TO SKATE OLD-SCHOOL 70'S STYLE AND DO IT WELL. HE WAS QUICK TO LEARN WHATEVER I SHOWED HIM. HE TOLD ME HOW IMPORTANT IT WAS TO HIM TO BE ABLE TO DO MOST OF HIS OWN SKATING IN THE FILM, THAT HE REALLY WANTED TO PULL IT OFF, HE DIDN'T WANT TO BE JUST ANOTHER ACTOR.

—Stacy

When they put my extensions in my hair I immediately thought "OK so I pretty much look like a chick" and the result was this picture. JCR

I know a shot of myself of that age — you could cut my head off and put it on his body and it would be a perfect match—
Shy

When I got the part my biggest fear was not being able to look like I could skate and surf. I snowboarded alot and surfed a little but skating was a brand new adventure. About 2 weeks into training I realized that it might be possible. I trained everyday both surfing and skating which was really where I got to know my character.
JCR

John's physical ability on a board impressed me..!
Sf. Aliza

18

John was the first actor to make it over the light, we all soon followed. But I think John set the standard for all of us, especially with skating.

– Mike

John was a super dedicated athlete — really trained hard. He got so good — did so much of his own skating — but about week 3, he sprained his ankle BAD. Then reinjured it. He really couldn't skate and we still had 2 months to go. One day outside the pool, he and I both started anew) it was such a drag. I said — maybe if you stay off for a month — you can SKATE the DOGBOWL. He did — and check it out that's him SKATING OVER THE LIGHT — RIGHT UP TO CAMERA!
– CAT

Learning to ride a bike down stairs with a surf board in one hand was a lot harder than it looks. SCR

19

Mike trained so hard — I had to tell him "SID ISN'T SUPPOSED TO ~~BE THAT~~ GOOD A ~~SKATER~~ SKATER, dude!"

CAT

Sid, the character Michael plays is a composite of a number of characters we all knew back in the day. Michael ~~brings~~ brings so much life to him; he's compassionate, funny and in many ways the glue that ~~keeps~~ tries to hold everyone together.

— Stacy

X18:45:27:08   KU 77 2974 7742 01 B2
12:03:25:21:

TELL ME I'M A GREAT SKATER!

MICHAEL ANGARANO AS SID

This day was actually Heath's last day of filming, so I just decided to put all of his wig/wardrobe stuff on and do a little ~~Heath~~ impersonation. Emile did a real good Heath/Skip impression too, but mine ~~still~~ was the shit as you can see... — ~~Mike~~

Me & Miss America having some fun, she was the best. We had some fun rehearsing our scenes if ya know what I mean... ☺

— Mike

I think Mike is way talented and FUNNY. However, in this photo, he was actually posing for Teen Vogue. Emile.

21

the most crucial element was
capturing the energy that Kathy had.
It was also nice playing a character
that was younger than myself
and slightly more innocent. 😊

Kathy Alva told me that she was at
a party one night with her sort-of
boyfriend — who sounded like kind of
a dud — he went home early.
Jay Adams moved in and they ended
up together in the same room as
Tony and his girlfriend. This story
inspired the "give me kitty" scene. CAT

NIKKI REED
AS

KATHY ALVA

I remember looking in the mirror every day and thinking,
"God I look just like my mother when she was
"groovin'" in the 70's.

X03:19:22:17   KU.04 5786 4565+06 C2 X   :   KU.04 4350 7674+02 (
     16:16:11:19.   13:41:06:12.

obviously
I had NOTHING
to complain
about while
shooting this
film -Nikki

23

this guy is the
reincarnation of
my idol/mentor
A.K.A. "the player"
He was the man
& a great surfer
too.

with
respect,   R.I.P.

24

JOHNNY KNOXVILLE AS **TOPPER BURKS**

Limo intoxication. Thinking? Nahh...
— Emile

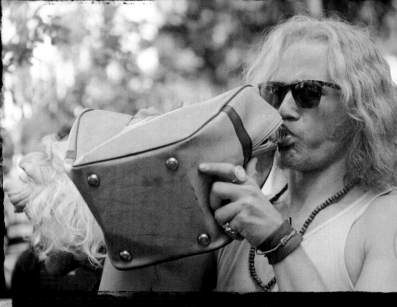

Taken from the film

HEATH LEDGER AS SKIP

↑
I think I finally learned how to act in this scene. Just reacting to Heath was all I could do. —John

One of the cool things about Heath playing the part of Skip is that he didn't need to be indoctrinated into the culture. he is a surfer and he is a skater so he already knew the code of ethics. He didn't have to act it because he's already lived it. —Stacy

When I first met with Skip, he told me he wanted Heath Ledger to play him. I thought he was delusional. "No fuckin' way Heath Ledger is playing Skip in my movie." cut to: 2 months later, we're making prosthetic teeth for Heath and he is kicking ass! —Cat

G. Alva

P.S. Skip got the major upgrade of the century.

26

ENGBLOM

I KEEP TELLING MY WIFE SHE'S SLEEPING
WITH HEATH LEDGER — SHE NEED GLASSES —
Stacy —

HEATH TOOK ME
ASIDE AND IMPARTED
IT'S ALL NONSENSE,
NOTHING IS REAL,

Craig Stecyk

pacific ocean park

EXT. P.O.P. — DAY
Enclosed within a jail cell of broken pilings is this secret SURF SPOT. Furious sets roll in like horizontal tornadoes - 8 foot swells charge into the Cove, causing hundreds of loosened pilings to sway like dislodged buoys. Atop the pier, rusted rides shift with each passing wave — creating a low creaking moan.

TO SEE THE P.O.P. SET & TO FOLLOW EMILE (JAY)
THROUGH THE PATH SKATING WITH A SURFBOARD, LOOKIN'
OVER & TO SEE CRAIG IN THE BACKGROUND
DRESSED AS A BUM. WAS AN EYE OPENER.
WHAT THAT SMALL GROUP OF KIDS
AND TEAM DID FOR ALL OF US.
EVEN THOUGH IT WAS JUST FOR
THEM SELVES AT THE TIME.
                              — LANCE

Lance Mountain,
SkateCam operator

30

We scooted all the wooden piers up
and down the California coast and
ended up at Imperial Beach,
south of San Diego. Chris Gorak,
our production designer, drew
some great sketches and designed
a way to piece the P.O.P. together
by building a section of the broken
down pier at Imperial Beach,
a section of sidewalk in Venice,
and pulling it all together with
computer-generated visual effects
by a Venice company, GRAY MATTER.
—CAT

Taken from the film

BEFORE

GI by Gray Matter

AFTER

LORDS OF DOGTOWN

Benefitting
Imperial Beach and
South County

Amount Spent

$ _____

DOGTOWN DOLLAR

852856

31

The Art Department did concept sketches, built a model, and drafted blueprints for the section of P.O.P. that we built at Imperial Beach

CAT

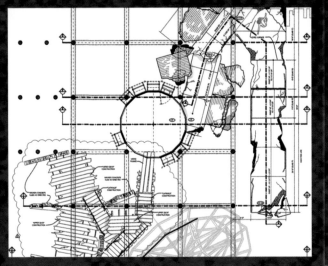

Courtesy Cale Wilbanks

Courtesy Cale Wilbanks

WE BOUGHT THIS FERRIS WHEEL FROM A GUY IN INDIANAPOLIS ON EBAY... WE TRUCKED IT OUT HERE, SET IT UP IN THE SAND, BEAT THE SHIT OUT OF IT.
– LARS PETERSON, CONSTRUCTION CO-ORDINATOR

Elliot Davis, our
Cinematographer.
His hair matches
the set!
CAT

pacific ocean

To the Police & Neighbors of P.O.P.
It was a nuisance. To the winos,
drug addicts, perverts and pyros
it was a safe haven. To the
surfers who lived for this surf
spot it was a paradise worth
defending from all outsiders through
intimidation, vandalism, territorial
markings and physical harm -

Jim Mui
REDDOG
2005

park

PACIFIC OCEAN PARK... IT WAS LIKE THE DISNEYLAND OF THE PACIFIC. IT JUST WENT FROM A PARADISE TO A WASTELAND. YOU COULDN'T GET CLOSE TO THE PLACE WITHOUT HAVIN' LIKE A ROCK THROWN AT YOU. IF YOU DIDN'T HAVE AN IN, YOU DIDN'T WANT TO BE THERE – CAUSE YOU'D GET YOUR BUTT KICKED. – RAY FLORES

Taken from the film

Taken from the film

Legendary big-wave surfer Brock Little (right) got hair extensions and grew a fat mustache to double for Chino — played by Vincent Laresca. CAT

"I WAS TRYING TO FIGURE OUT HOW TO GET THE SHOT OF HITTING THE PIER AFTER OUR SET BROKE WITH THE FOAM RUBBER PYLON. AND BROCK CAME UP TO ME AND SAID "I'LL JUST HIT THE REAL PIER. HOW BAD CAN IT BE?" AS BROCK SAID AFTER HE DID IT, "THAT HURT LIKE A MOTHERFUCKER."
— TOMMY HARPER
STUNT CO-ORDINATOR

PRO SURFER GAVIN SUTHERLAND DOUBLED JAY
HE RIPPED IT UP ON THE 70'S SINGLE FIN

Taken from the film

Don King and Sonny Miller are two of the most famous surf photographers on the planet. Sonny had to make special housings for the cameras so the "wimps" could watch the video playback from the pier. That's Brock Little holding onto my raft — ready to save me if a rogue wave rolls in. CAT

We'd be watching dailies, and I hear someone say "WAVE coming!" — then hear a gurgling sound and the rest of the shot would be an upside-down shot of the wave-runner drivers legs. We'd put a black dot on those shots so we'd know not to show that part to Catherine.

— Nancy Richardson
editor

CONTAMINATED!

I heard Tommy Harper got poisoned from the water and was puking and had diarrhea for like 48 hours. We were all like, "Fuck going in the water after that!" Tommy was our sacrificial lamb. He's 4th from the right. — Emile

we only had 5 days to shoot all the P.O.P. stuff and we got SHUT DOWN one of the days due to the high "FECAL COUNT" in the water! CAT

THE FLYING FILIPINO
VICTOR'S SURF DOUBLE
ALVIN ZALAMEA

PRO SURFER
BRAD GERLACH

BONEYARD CREW

Collins
Griffin is a man in
the truest sense of the
word. With barely socks
on, he rode a Venice
back alley for 10 hours
straight. His feet were
black and blue bruised,
but he had a strong sense
of duty to skateboarding,
and laughed maniacally,
took a drag of his cigarette
and came back for more.
— Emile

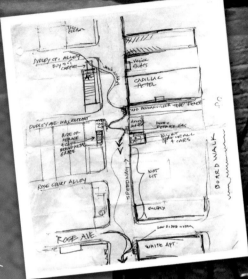

we got to shoot
in the real Speedway
Alley in Venice, a block
away from the old
P.O.P. pier location
CAT

I WAS SKATING FROM 3PM TO
6AM ON MY 21ST B-DAY BARE
FOOT AND BLOODY. HARDEST
NIGHT OF SHOOTING. THIS IS
ONE I CAN SAY I AM TRULY
PROUD OF. — GRIFFIN COLLIN
JAY ADAMS SKATE DOUBLE.

THE HOOD

the Z-boyz told me that when they skated, even early in the A.M., he made a LOT OF ~NOISE~, crashing into CARS, smashing TRASH CANS, TERRORIZING THE NEIGHBORHOOD. So, we made him a path.... CAT

When I was directing the RATTY SLAP scene
in Venice, Emile started sassing me back.
I stepped up to his face and said
"You wanna take this out on the beach!*/*/"
I was about to hit him — then I noticed
Heath was just staring at me. I ran around the
block to calm down. I guess the testosterone
was getting to me. — CAT

I had my wetsuit around
my ankles and barely got
it off in time to answer
my cell phone. Ginger was on
one line requesting my presence
on the set & immediatly
she yelled into my ear that
Catherine was running around
the block in Venice (a few blocks
from me) screaming "Are
there any new skaters on
the set? I jammed over
there pronto.

've discussed the chip
bowl dialogue, immediatly
resolved the dilemma
and diffused the ticking
time bomb of tension.
— T. Alva

44

THE NEIGHBORS REALLY HATED US FOR THIS KIND OF STUFF

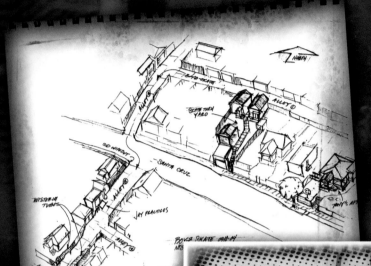

Taken from the film

bombing
BICKNELL HILL

This was one of my favorite ~~stuff~~ times
here. Forget story, plot, character –
just shut up and ride it like a wave.
— Emil

praying
the movie
works.
Emil

SEEING THE SHOP FELT LIKE DEJA VU. IT WAS NOT EXACT, BUT HAD THE FEEL OF THE OLD PIG STY.

zephyr shop: workspace

ET REALLY, IN THE END,
WAS ABOUT WORK AND
THE LOVE YOU HAVE
FOR THE JOB. IT'S
DIRTY, FILTHY,
UNHEALTHY –
BUT THE END PRODUCT
IS SO SEXY.

YOU THINK YOU KNOW
WHAT IT'S GOING TO
DO – HOW IT'S GOING
TO BE YOUR DANCE
PARTNER. YOUR
LIFE'S FULL FOR A
FEW MOMENTS. THEN
YOU THINK, JUST
LIKE GIRLFRIENDS,
THE NEXT ONE'S
GOING TO BE
BETTER.

BRIAN ZARATE

ELDEN HENSON

THE KIDS WERE REALLY
GREAT. THEY REALLY
KIND OF LOCKED INTO
WHAT IT WAS ABOUT.
SOME TIMES IT WAS
ALMOST TOO REAL.
I HAD TO GO OUTSIDE.
F--- THIS IS 2005
NOT 1975—

by Catherine Hardwicke

I GOT SOMETHING
BETTER THAN CASH –
URETHANE SKATEBOARD
WHEELS

SOME OF THESE GUYS COULDN'T MAKE IT OVER THE TOP_ NO NAMES
—ED

ELLIOT DAVIS,
DIRECTOR OF PHOTOGRAPHY

SKATING BANKS

When all of us were growing up during the Dogtown days, surfing Bay Street and skateboarding Bicknell Hill and the local school playgrounds, we were always being told by outsiders, especially East Coasters, that there was no culture in Los Angeles. It was felt that LA was a cultural wasteland. LORDS OF DOGTOWN is a testament to how wrong they all were. There was culture out here. The problem was that it was unrecognizable at the time because it was a new form of urban culture. It was something people hadn't yet seen. — STACY PERALTA

Ouww my nuts!
— Emile

Lance Cam

LIPSTICK CAM
SHOT OF URETHANE
WHEELS GRIPPING
THE BANKS

by Catherine Hardwicke

Taken from the film

aspects of the DOWNHILL

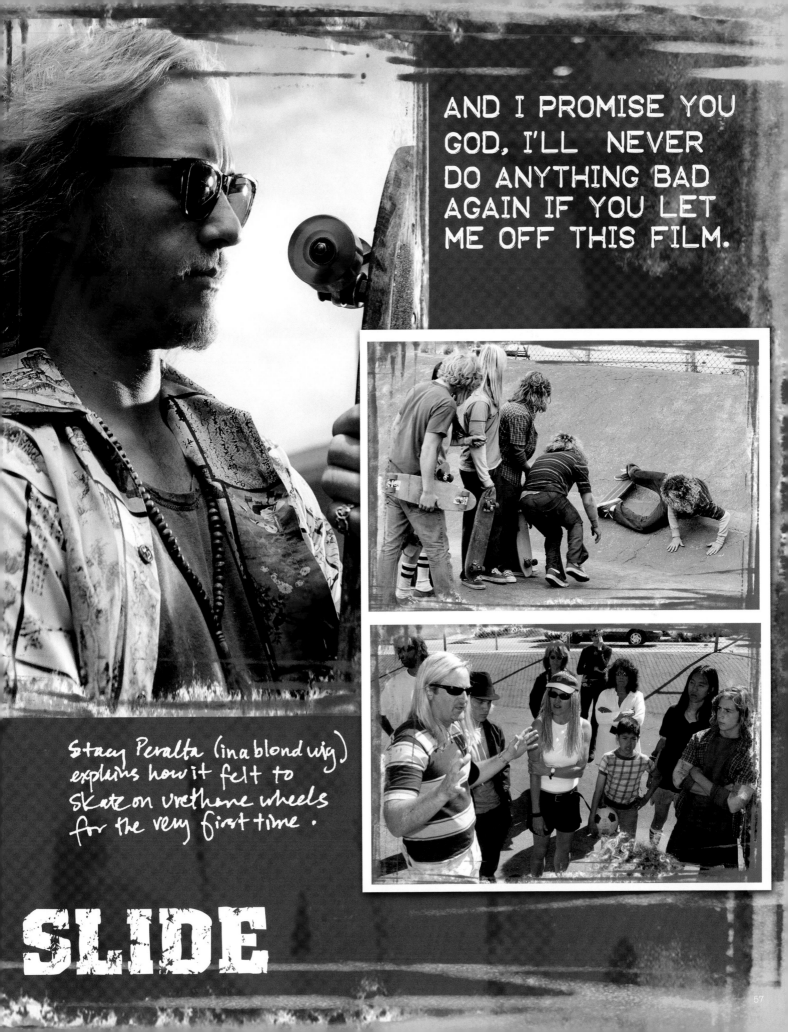

AND I PROMISE YOU GOD, I'LL NEVER DO ANYTHING BAD AGAIN IF YOU LET ME OFF THIS FILM.

Stacy Peralta (in a blond wig) explains how it felt to skate on urethane wheels for the very first time.

SLIDE

100%
RAW DITCH
SKATING...

WE CAME HERE WHEN WE WERE
SHUT OUT OF THE OCEAN.
OUT OF ONE SEWER AND INTO
ANOTHER.— ED.

BEING a MODERN SKATEBOARDER
WITH OLD SCHOOL ROOTS, THIS MOVIE
MADE ALL OF US LEARN A STYLE
OF SKATEBOARDING THAT WE TOOK
TO HEART. — STEVE BADILLO

Lance
Mountain,
Brad
Gerlach,
and
Stacy double
Bradlee
Coleman.

61

WEAR 'EM WITH PRIDE

SKATEBOARD COMPETITION

INTERNATIONAL SKATEBOARDING COMMISSION

ISC

FREESTYLE SLALOM

MEN'S AND WOMEN'S

CASH AND PRIZES

DEL MAR

...OR WE'LL RIP 'EM OFF YOUR BONY LITTLE BACKS.

I GUESS THE ROAD TO HELL REALLY IS PAVED WITH GOOD INTENTIONS.

Biniak looks like he's opening a little too wide for my comfort.
-Emile

63

DEL
MAR

Wild one Catherine Hardwicke contemplates
the upcoming scene, and uses her visionary
intellect to make us dirty little skate gromits
more hardcore, hardcore and historical.
When a gromit falls she yells like Cleopatra
"Up, another!" When a gromit cries she comforts.
— Emile

We finally landed on a location that gave us the Spanish Style backdrop that 'Del Mar Fairgrounds' required. The challenge with Del Mar set was to design the low tech ramps and platforms of the original event in such a way that they were a bit more skater friendly for the several days of shooting and repeatable skate choreography without losing the cheesy originality. In other words making sure skaters didn't wreck on loose screws, dusty plywood or bite it in a row of hay bales at the bottom of the slalom ramp when ripping it up with the retro skateboards.

— CHRIS GORAK,
Production Designer

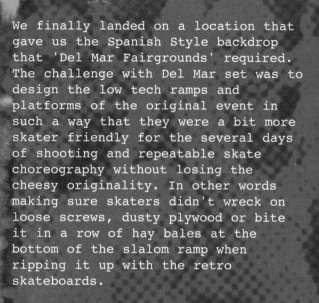

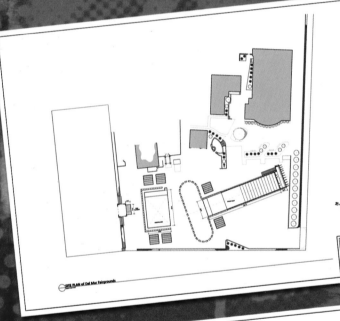

I think we all tried to kreate
most of the poses, but I
ended up looking like
some hippy acid head
who fell asleep dreaming
of whatever... Mike on
MY left looks like a
fucking GEEK though
haha. Who on earth is
Don Ngyune (spelled that
wrong, sorry DON) looking
at?
— Emile

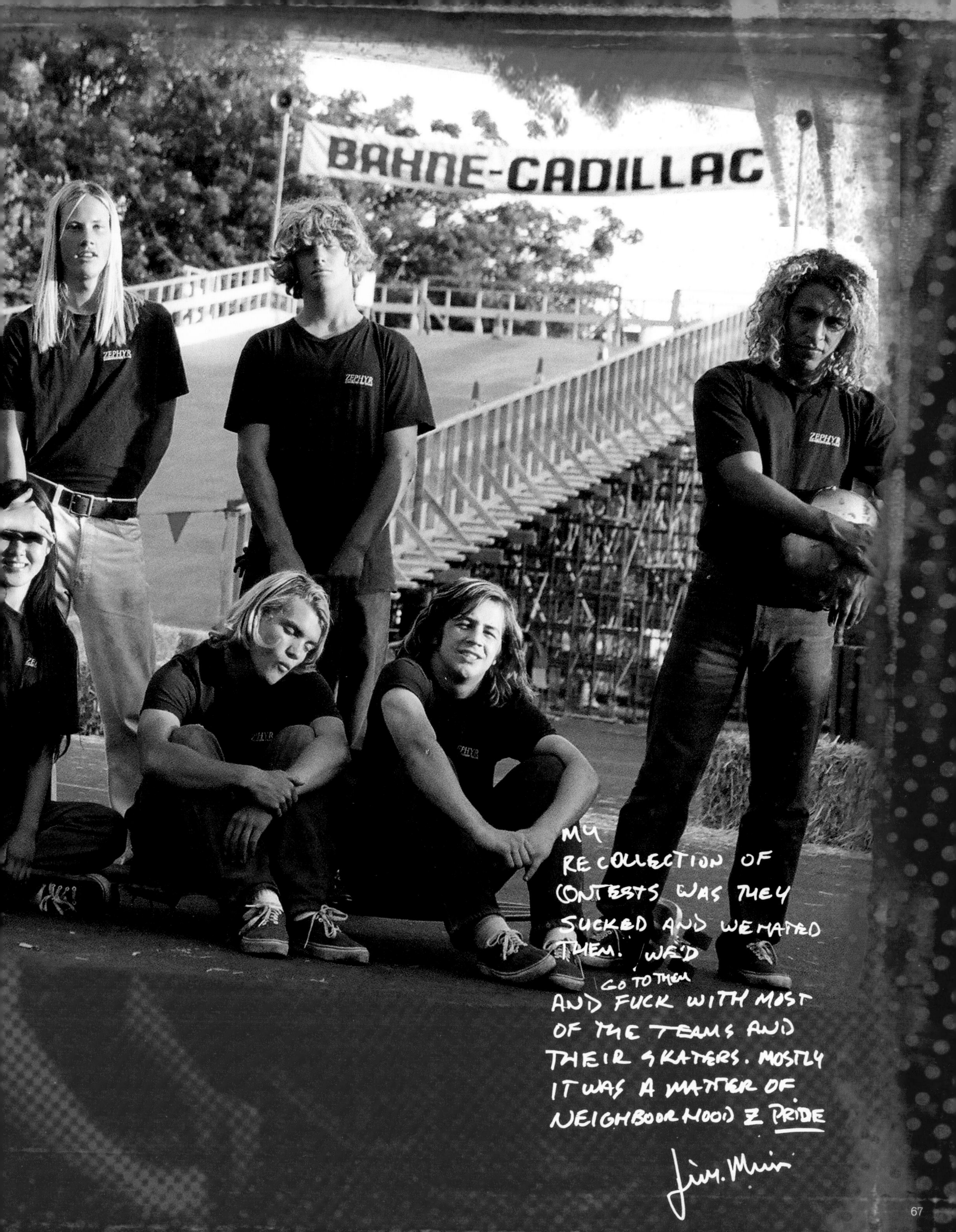
BAHNE-CADILLAC
ZEPHYR

MY RECOLLECTION OF CONTESTS WAS THEY SUCKED AND WE HATED THEM. WE'D GO TO THEM AND FUCK WITH MOST OF THE TEAMS AND THEIR SKATERS. MOSTLY IT WAS A MATTER OF NEIGHBOORHOOD Z PRIDE

Jim. Muir

One day at skate boot camp, I looked at our trainer, Steve Badillo (dressed in hip hop baggy pants and a backwards hat) and said: "You're gonna play Ty Page!" I don't think he believed me at first, but I kept telling him he better start practicing his handstands & daffies. Now, whenever he sees the movie - he says he likes it, but there should be more of TY PAGE. CAT

Doing handstands and 360 spins are damn hard. Respect to Ty Page and Russ Howell.

STEVE BADILLO

After months of being repeatedly flogged by the half animal, Steve Badillo and outrageous Tony Alva in skate training, and overcoming a major back trauma as a result of which they almost ejected me from the movie like a crapped out VHS tape, I miraculously make my comeback and land my Royal Christie... look ma, no hands! Uhhh........ (the game) -Emile

JAY ADAMS

HE DIDN'T DO A HANDSTAND, AN L-SIT, OR A SINGLE WHEELIE... HELL, HE DIDN'T DO A SINGLE COMPULSORY TRICK.

This was the first time we, as Actors, were truly proud of eachother. VE.

THE ENTIRE ENTERPRISE HAS REALLY BROUGHT MANY OF US BACK TOGETHER AND STRENGTHENED OUR RELATIONSHIPS, ESPECIALLY TONY AND I. BACK IN THE DAY, HE AND I WERE NEVER CLOSE. WE SKATED TOGETHER A LOT BUT WE WERE NEVER CLOSE. THIS CURRENT EXPERIENCE HAS HAD A PROFOUND EFFECT ON OUR RELATIONSHIP AS IT'S ALLOWED US TO GET TO KNOW EACH OTHER AS MEN. —Stacy

Animal IN FULL SLIDE, pounding wood —Emile

TONY ALVA

706
Cadillac
Wheels

I was watching Tony give Victor tips
on how to skate his Del Mar routine.
Even his skate double, Adam Alfaro, was
having a hard time nailing Tony's style.
Then I realized — Nobody can skate more
like Tony than Tony! So he put on a
wig and a Zephyr shirt and blew us away!

CAT

Catherine asked Tony and I to
re-create our Del Mar runs.
We costumed up; wigs, shoes,
straight-leg cords and small
thin boards. During the my
run I could feel the heat
coming off the wooden platform,
and I could hear the crowd hoots
from the surrounding crowd and
I could hear Alva yelling me on.
The experience was so surreal
I felt like I had stepped
back in time.
                    —Stacy

Probably one of the
most nerve-racking
scenes for me. Having
to recreate what Stacy
did perfectly while
he is standing there
watching!! I couldn't do
justice.
              JCR

The real Stacy showed us all up, he's still
    got it... —Mike

72

STACY
PERALTA

WILL IT BE ALL OF YOU?

NO WE DID NOT RIP THIS MOVE OFF FROM "POOTY TANG"!

Heath is ready to take on all of the God Squad & more lets git it on!
Ct. Ahva

THE BELT THING CAME AFTER A GUY TRIED TO STIFF US FOR GLOSS JOBS, THEN TOOK THE BOARDS WITHOUT PAYING — I SOLD ALL THE BOARDS LATER.

TONY ALVA
USED GOGGLES TO CHECK OUT POOLS FOR TRANSITIONS, CRACKS, ETC.

Hey Tony,
Can You Fix this thing?

YOUR POOL HAS BEEN
TONY ALVA APPROVED

100% *Alva*

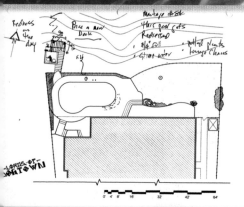

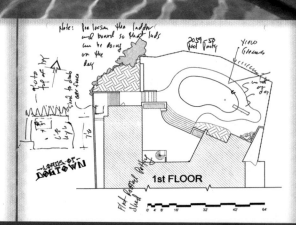

1st FLOOR

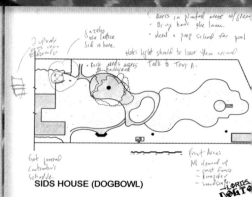

SIDS HOUSE (DOGBOWL)

Tony Alva couldn't believe that we would be legally allowed to see people's swimming pools. and then pick the one's he wanted to skate — legally empty them — legally skate. GORAK

DRAIN IT!

TOXIC WASTE BATH

Cheyne Magnussen plays Jim "Red Dog" Muir.
He surfs for Quicksilver and lives in Maui.
There wasn't cash to pay for Cheyne's hotel
the whole time we were filming — we were budgetted
for LOCAL HIRES. So I called up Muir and asked
if he had an extra bed. I told him that if he
didn't let Cheyne crash there, we might have to
cut Red Dog out of the movie. Needless to say,
Cheyne moved in with Jim and it was a beautiful thing —
CAT

Tommy Harper don't raise
no PUSSIES!
His 14 yr.old Kid RILEY
doubled for SID. Riley did
one of these falls and
I said "that looked pretty
good - I think we got
it." I didn't want Riley
to get hurt. Tommy
looked at me and said -
"He's going again!"
CAT

When I DID THIS FALL, Everyone thought I had died. I walked
away without a scratch..... only a sprained ankle.
— Riley Harper

79

Sometimes we were like,
out of my FACE And le[

"Get that damn camera
me 5K8!" —Smile

TONY ALVA AND TOMMY HARPER,
STUNT CO-ORDINATOR

stunts go deep in the Harper
gene pool. Tommy's grandad
crashed cars for the
Keystone cops. CAT

I DON'T THINK WE USED ANY LIGHTS IN THE
POOL.   "DAYS OF HEAVEN" DOESN'T HA
ANY THING ON US.
ED

Occasionally that pole camera
would smack someone in the face.
It was almost like jousting.
Emile

ONLY WAY TO GET THE CAMERA WHERE IT
HAD TO BE. THE RIGHT TOOL FOR THE RIGHT
JOB_ ED

Sequence photographed by Lance-Cam.

PERALTA

Brad told me he started skating right after he saw "Dogtown and Z-Boys." After seeing him skate I believed him. He has within him the complete physical DNA make-up of a 70's skateboarder; beautiful style and flow, great speed and finesse, the Look-hair, pants etc... ...and just the attitude from that time. It's as if the film crew reached back in time to find him. I couldn't have been too more stoked with his skating —

Stacy

BRADLEE COLEMAN,
ONE OF THE SKATE
DOUBLES FOR STACY
PERALTA

JAY BOY

JAY DOUBLE - GRIFFIN COLLINS -

GONZALES POOL...

He never let us down. Grif. Dog is no joke.

O. Alva

GREAT STUFF —

GETTING THE CAMERA IN THE RIGHT PLACE AT THE RIGHT TIME — THERE'S THE RUB. SOMETIMES YOU JUST COULDN'T DO IT AND OTHER TIMES IT WAS, WELL, JUST PURE MAGIC. — ED.

ELLIOT DAVIS,
DIRECTOR OF PHOTOGRAPHY

87

MAD DOG

Watching Alf skate in pools was a treat. He adapted to the small boards very easily. Brad also had a natural ability to skate vert & street on primitive gear. It was amazing. T. Alva

ADAM ALFARO.

"Adam Alfaro
made me look
sooooo good. If
you read this Adam...
... THANK YOUS"
                    -vic

89

I felt bad for Catherine when shooting the party. After a few hours on the first day of shooting it, it definitely turned into a real party, and when you have like 70 extras + skaters + surfers, it gets kinda hard to control them. But Catherine was tough and spanked anyone who got outta line...

— Mike

I HEARD THERE WAS A **PARTY** IN MY FAVORITE SURF GHETTO

he looks crazy enough to drink his own piss - Emile

It was so hard to stay serious when I was acting with Johnny Knoxville. He's so funny. Especially with a wig and Fedora.
—v.z

JAY

You couldn't handle her.

STACY

Oh? And you can?!

JAY

Apparently so.

DESERT PIPES

Originally this stunt was an *Alva* innovation similar to the 1st Air. We needed something big & dynamic for second unit footage. the boys (John & Craig) stepped it up once again. ~~POW!!~~ take that.

— T. Alva

FLYING IN ZERO
WORTH THE POTENTIAL CONCRETE

Man, ~~one dude~~ Craig took like 3 slams
HARD in a ROW, but he got up and kept
hitting it over the gap until his
mission was accomplished. —Emile.

THE PIPE DAY WAS COOL.
I GOT TO WORK WITH
MY SON, HE WAS A
VATO SKATER AND THE
CAMERA WAS THE SIZE
OF A LIPSTICK CASE. WHY
DIDN'T THEY HAVE THIS
EARLIER. — LANCE

Lance Mountain follows with
lipstick camera.

GRAVITY—
PITFALL ON

— Emile.

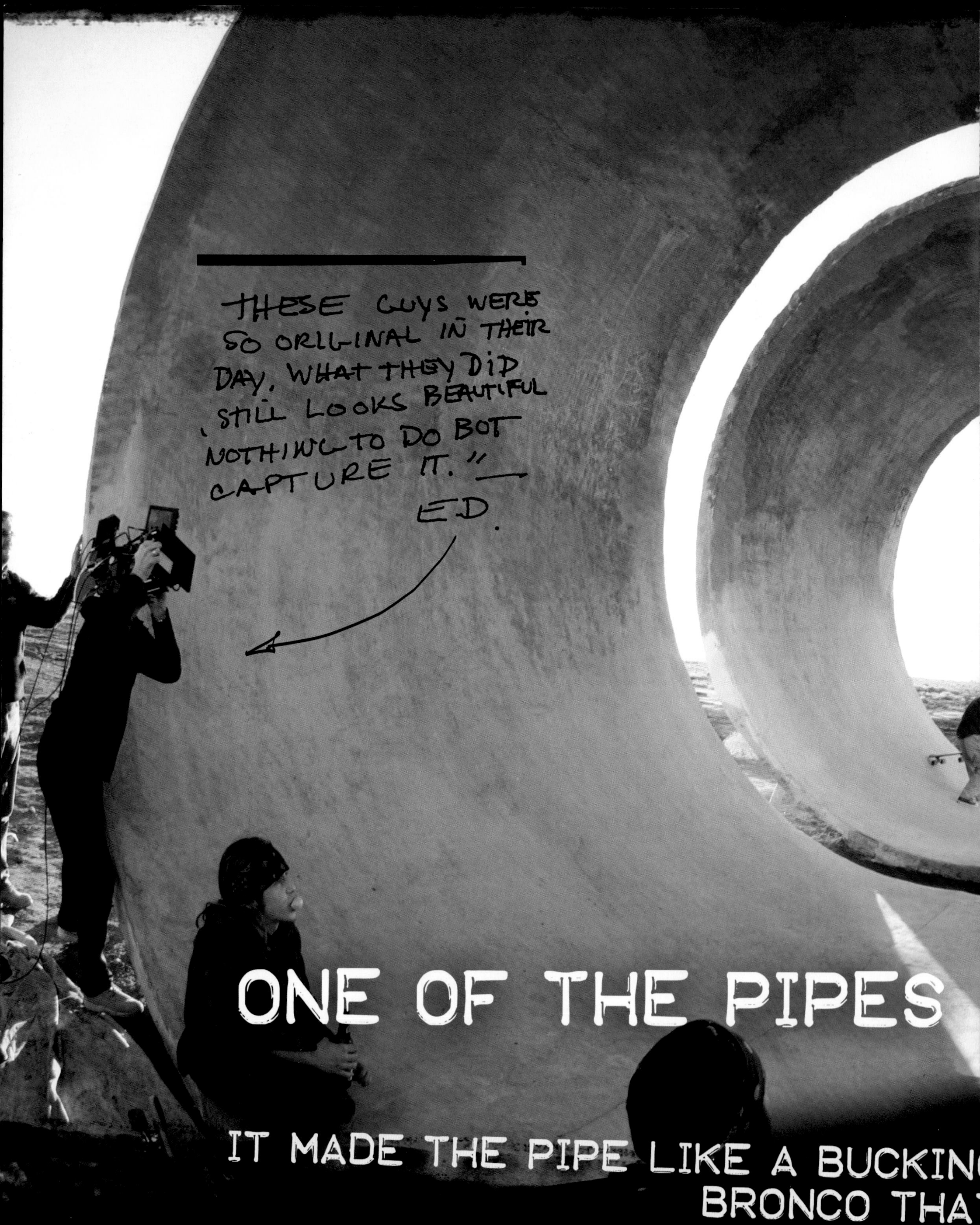

ONE OF THE PIPES

IT MADE THE PIPE LIKE A BUCKIN
BRONCO THA

HAD A HUGE
SPEED BUMP
AT THE BOTTOM.

TRIED TO MAKE YOUR ASS FALL HARD. — Emile

THE PIPES ARE SO IMPORTANT TO
SKATEBOARDING IN THE 70'S. I'm
GLAD WE WERE ABLE TO RECREATE
THE FEEL OF DISCOVERY AND CREATIVE
PROCESS OF THOSE EARLY SKATEBOARDERS.
— STEVE BADILLO

HERE I AM READY FOR
COMBAT PHOTOGRAPHY

E.D.

101

WORLD PROFESSIONAL SKATEBOARD COMPETITION

SHOGO

Skateboarding's been great. I'm thinking about buying a new Trans-Am... black on black, with some big fat tires in the back.

Taken from the film

Long Beach Auditorium had something like 1000 seats and we could afford something like 500 extras. So a lot of the seats were filled with legless inflatable people wearing wigs & 70's shirts... At least they showed up every day... CA

Long Beach was the largest scale set we used and I would sneak up to the spot lights and follow random people with the giant light shining down. SCK

Tyson has his own website. He taught himself to skate and gets mad if you try to take away his skateboard.

CAT

105

                    STACY
Do you guys skate with Tony any
more?

                    JAY

The dude's competing with the sun
for the center of the universe.

Stacy laughs and walks away. Jay turns to Sid.

                JAY (CONT'D)
Stacy looks like a stock car.

CHRIS CHAPUT
AS RUSS HOWELL

STACY
Hey, Tony. Looks like
it's gonna be you or me.

TONY
Oh no, it's not. it's me.

this encounter between
Stacy & I is based on
the Carlsbad Hang ten
World Pro championship.
the dialogue is the same
but the end result was
very different. Victor
delivered the line with
confidence.

CJ. Alva
"class among gruel"

DOG BOWL

Shirtless Mafia, on the weekends we hit the town haarrrd.
— Emile

The Dog Bowl was a well crafted machine. The most perfect pool ever created that. I hear they moved the coping to some of Mexico. — John

was soon ripped apart.
Pool in Mexico. The legend lives on in the heart

THE DOGBOWL TOOK EVERYONE
OUT, SO ALVA WAS DRESSED AS
AN ALVA DOUBLE ONE DAY..
HIS STYLE WAS REALLY QUITE
CLOSE TO THE REAL THING.
— LANCE

SHOOTING IN THE DOG-BOWL WAS A
CROSS BETWEEN COMBAT PHOTOJOURNALISM
AND MOUNTAIN CLIMBING__, ED

Tyler was my ~~other~~ character's other double. He's shown
here demonstrating his commitment — wheels out and his
back foot is still firmly planted. Great form. — Stacy

LANCE MOUNTAIN
TAKES A BREAK FROM SHOOTING
THE DOG BOWL

THE FIRST DAY IT FELT
LIKE I WAS AT FOOTBALL
TRY-OUTS. I HAD TO PROVE
TO THEM I COULD CARRY
THE CAMERA, FOLLOW THE
SKATERS AND GET SHOTS
THAT IMPRESSED THEM.
BIG 35mm WITH ALL
SORTS OF BATTERIES AND
REMOTE HOOK UPS. DOGGIE
CAM SOME SORT OF BODY
HARNESS WITH A CAMERA
THAT WAS 10 POUNDS HEAVY
UP ON A STICK 4 FEET
ABOVE MY HEAD. AND I
WAS TRYING TO GET THE
SKATER IN FRAME. 3 OTHER
CAMERA MEN WERE THERE

SAYING THEY COULD DO IT.
I WON'T GET THIS JOB.
I KNOW NOTHING ABOUT
CAMERA'S I DON'T EVEN
KNOW HOW TO FOCUS, &
THEY WERE ALL LETTING
ME KNOW THEY KNEW.
ONE ROLLER BLADER SAID HE
COULD CARRY TWO CAMERA'S
AND ROLL IN AND OUT
OF THE POOL FOLLOWING
THE SKATERS. I'M THINKING
HOW CAN I SNEAK A RUN
IN THE POOL WITH OUT
THE CAMERA BEFORE THEY
TELL ME TO GO HOME:
"WE HAVE A CAMERA MAN
WE DON'T NEED YOU."
        —LANCE

These dogs here were the well behaved ones. One dog bugged
out earlier and bit Tony Alva as he hit the coping on his
board. Needless to say, the dog was FIRED.
        —Emile

Vic got one
of his tds bit
aswell —Schu

10,000 HAND PLANTS
LATER

Adam Alfaro recreated the first air with style & grace. I'm still stoked on his performance so I went out and did my own version. —T. Alva

Tony will be doing this when he's sixty. —Stacy

BOWL

KU.77 0532 6844+12 A2
CAM:S16
08:13:38:25:

KU.04:8524 8504+01

13:14:53:01:

Taken from the film

RIDING THE REBUILT DOGBOWL WAS A DREAM
COME TRUE. ESPECIALLY CONSIDERING WE HELPED DESIGN AND BUILD IT.
I GOT TO SKATE IN MY NEW DESIGNS -- 21ST CENTURY. THAT, IN ITSELF,
WAS FUCKIN' GREAT. I'M STOKED.   TONY ALVA

"I'm the freshest thing in town."

This was one of the rare times the skactors were actually not in motion. There is even a slight chance they might be sober. K. Roth

Kenny Roth, Second A.D.

meet the SKACTORS

ska-ctor *n* (circa 2004) / (skack-ter) skaters, actors... um, it seems pretty self explanatory.

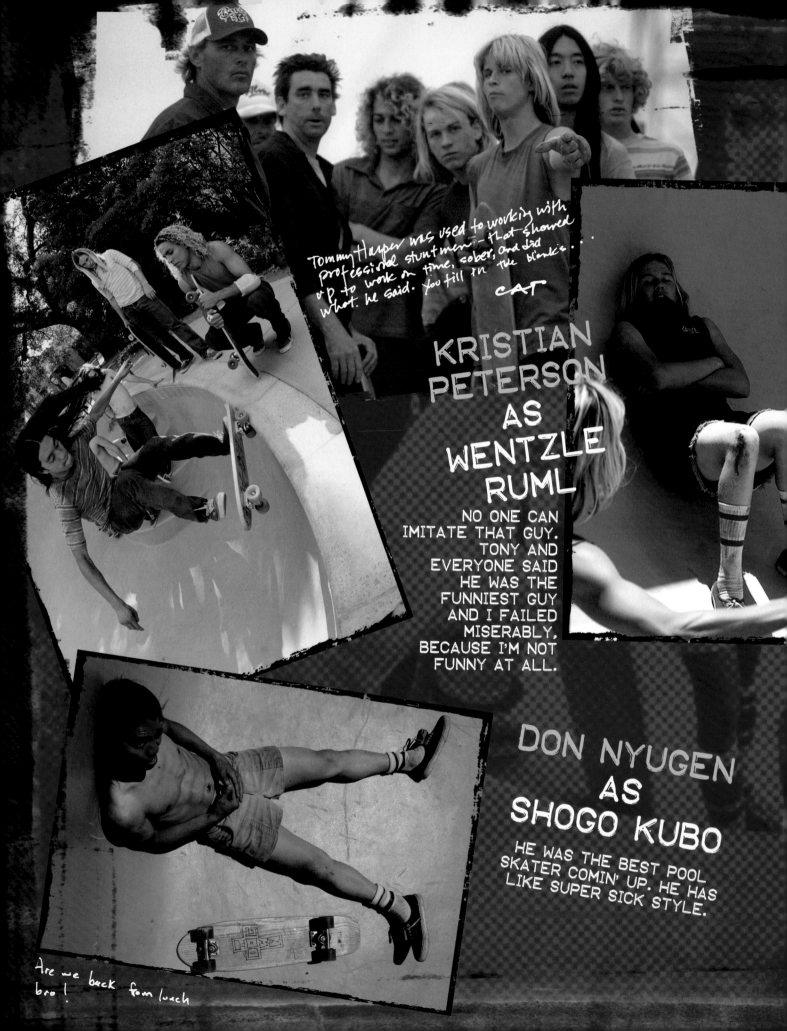

Tommy Harper was used to working with professional stuntmen - that showed up to work on time, sober, and did what he said. You fill in the blanks...
CAT

KRISTIAN PETERSON

AS

WENTZLE RUML

NO ONE CAN IMITATE THAT GUY. TONY AND EVERYONE SAID HE WAS THE FUNNIEST GUY AND I FAILED MISERABLY, BECAUSE I'M NOT FUNNY AT ALL.

DON NYUGEN

AS

SHOGO KUBO

HE WAS THE BEST POOL SKATER COMIN' UP. HE HAS LIKE SUPER SICK STYLE.

Are we back from lunch bro!

ERIC "TUMA" BRITTON
AS MARTY GRIMES

MARTY WAS PROBABLY THE ONLY BROTHER THAT SKATED FOR THE ZEPHYR TEAM IN THE 70'S ... I GREW UP IN VENICE, SO IT WAS NATURAL THAT I'D PLAY MARTY GRIMES IN THIS FILM. HE WAS KNOWN FOR THE WAY HE THREW HIS HANDS UP WHEN HE DID FRONTSIDE SLASHES.

Tuma can rip. Period.
– Emil

Rock N Roll!
A bunch of skate demons take a momentary pause from their death defying stunts to relax for a minute
Emile

119

CHEYNE MAGNUSSON
AS
JIM "RED DOG" MUIR

IT'S BIG SHOES TO FILL.

"EVERYBODY'S STYLE ON THE SET IS PRETTY MUCH EXACTLY LIKE IT WAS BACK THEN. IT'S LIKE STEPPIN' INTO THE "TWILIGHT ZONE."

HE'S ALMOST AS GOOD-LOOKIN' AS ME AND A WAY BETTER SURFER. PEOPLE WOULD COME UP TO US AND GO, "HEY IS THAT YOUR SON?"
– JIM MUIR

STEPHANIE LIMB AS PEGGY OKI

THEY TOLD ME SHE SMILED A LOT. THAT'S MY BIGGEST CHALLENGE.

ACTUALLY, WHAT CATHERINE TOLD ME WAS THAT I WAS THE FIRST SKACTRESS.

Girls who skate are soooo sexy
—Emile

Shit! That shit was lethal bro!

MIKE OGUS AS BOB "THE BULLET" BINIAK

THE BABES

IN THIS SCENE, REBECCA HAD TO HUG ONE OF THE BOYS. THEY WERE PRACTICALLY KILLING EACH OTHER TO GET THE PART. — NIKKI REED

if I pretend I'm not enjoying it... maybe she'll do it again -

RED DOG GETS SOME SKACTION.

SOFIA
VERGARA

REBECCA
DE MORNAY

Is it
weird that
I'm attracted
to my mom?
Emile

Cost-saving tip:
Use the same
actresses for
2 scenes —
CAT

Some things never
change

MELONIE DIAZ
AS BLANCA

AMERICA FERRARA
AS THUNDER MONKEY

THE HOMEGIRLS VS. THE MALIBABES

WE HAD OUR OWN COOL THRIFT STORE LOOK — THOSE GIRLS HAD JAGUARS AND PORSCHES.
— KATHY ALVA

Two super hotties! — Emily

SARAH BLAKELY — CARTWRIGHT
LAURA RAMS

INSIDE VIEW

ORIGINAL Z-BOYZ BOB BINIAK AND STACY PERALTA,
WITH JACK SMITH, WHO COMPETED AT DEL MAR IN
1975, AND BOB BINIAK SKACTOR, MIKE OGUS,

ALAN SARLO, ORIGINAL Z-BOY,
REN SMITH FELLOW REAL
ESTATE AGENT/SURFER, AND
DIRECTOR C. HARDWICKE.

CHRISTIAN HOSOI

Two weirdos bond.
- Emile

JIM "RED DOG" MUIR

-Jim needs to watch what he grabs -John

THANKS TO CATHERINE HARDWICKE FOR STEREOTYPING MY FUTURE ACTING CAREER AS A FUCKING RENTA-COP.

SKIPPER THOUGHT IT WAS POST MODERN SHAKESPEARE... YOU LITTLE KNOB-ROCKIN BUTT CLOWN

Craig Stecyk

A TALE OF TWO STECYKS

CRAIG STECYK

SO SKIP YOU READY? HUH?
SO SKIP YOU READY? HUH?
PERFECT.

PABLO SCHREIBER

When I realized that Biniak was going to play the restaurant manager, I thought "I can't just have Heath hit him—he's got to hit back. I mean, it's BINIAK!"
CAT

BOB BINIAK

RAY
FLORES

PAUL
CONSTANTINEAU

DAVID
HACKETT

STEVE
OLSON

SKIP & STECYK

TONY HAWK

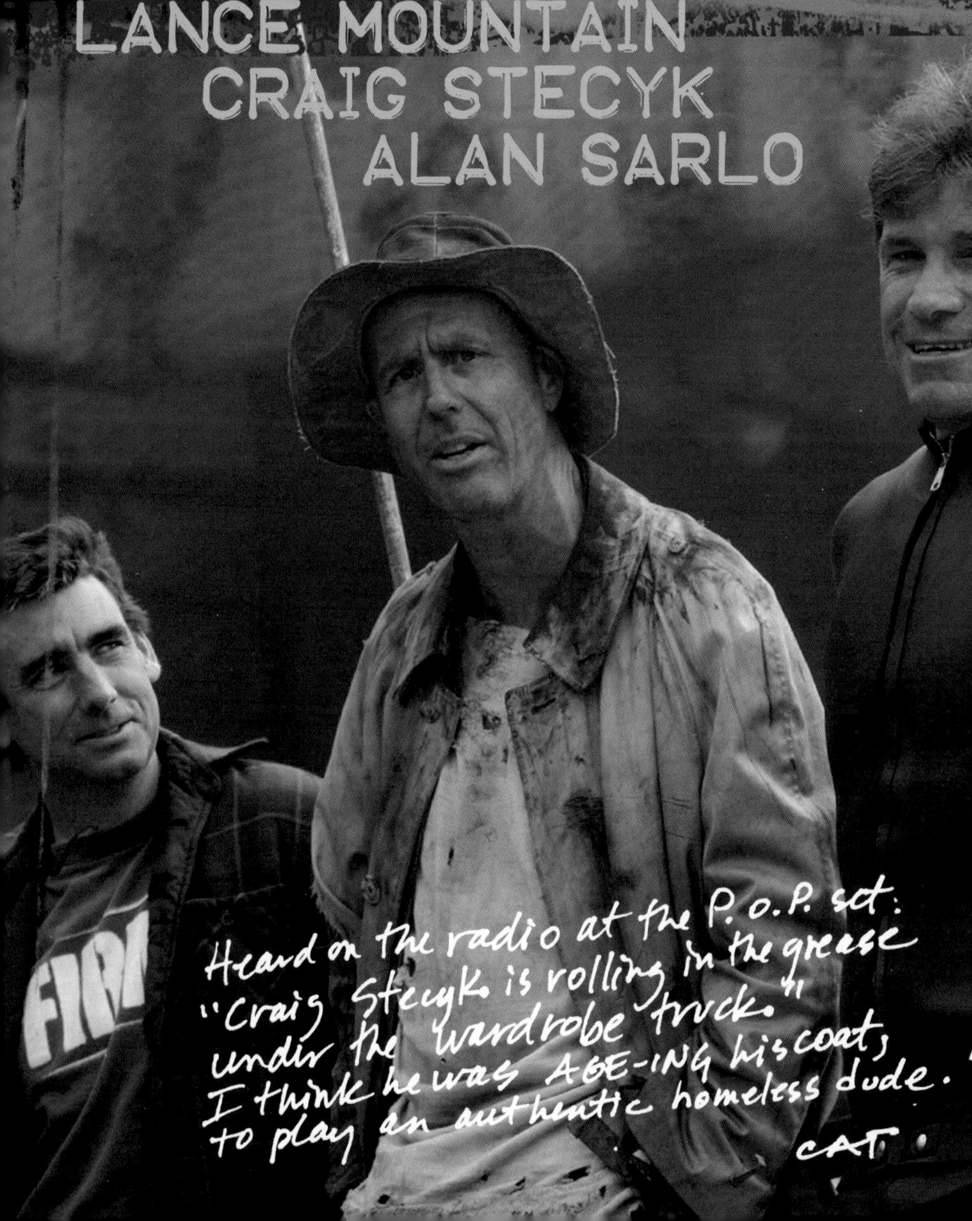

LANCE MOUNTAIN
CRAIG STECYK
ALAN SARLO

Heard on the radio at the P.O.P. set:
"Craig Stecyk is rolling in the grease
under the wardrobe truck."
I think he was AGE-ING his coat,
to play an authentic homeless dude.
CAT

WES
HUMPSTON

131

BACK IN THE DAY...

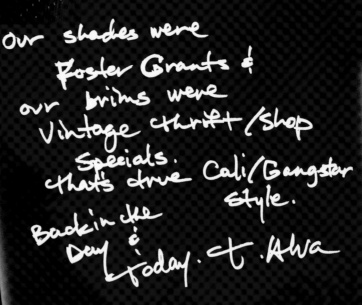

Our shades were Foster Grants & our brims were Vintage thrift/shop specials. that's true Cali/Gangster style. Back in the Day & today. - t. Alva

Thank
goodness
they aren't sitting down.
What's weirder— those old tiny
boards or those daisy dukes
a bunch of dudes are sporting!?
— Emile

LanceCam

I hated to do it, but one day I
had to institute the underwear
rule. there was just too much
CRACK showing. CAT

skate

SKIP TOLD ME THAT
GROWING UP IN VENICE
HE HAD ENOUGH TO
BUY ONE NEW PAIR OF
JEANS EVERY FALL.
HE'D WEAR THEM TO
SCHOOL ALL YEAR,
THEN IN SUMMER HE'D
CUT THEM OFF FOR
SHORTS. *CAT*

Cindy Evans, the costume designer,
had a whole crew in the basement
of SONY - "AGING" down the
jeans and T-shirts - making them
look old and ratty. There had to
be like 5 shirts that all looked the
same - for the stunts, etc.

VanG was a neighborhood store.
for the poor kids, they used to
sell them one shoe - if they
skated hard only their right foot,
for example. *CAT*

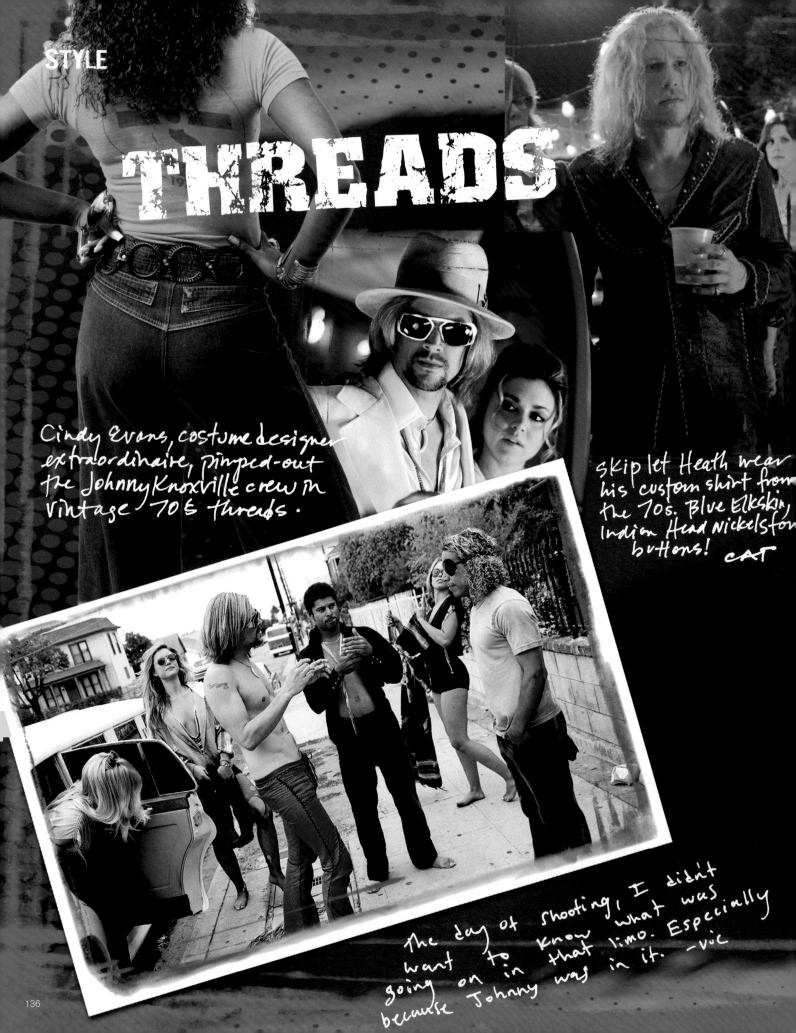

THREADS

Cindy Evans, costume designer extraordinaire, pimped-out the Johnny Knoxville crew in Vintage 70s threads.

Skip let Heath wear his custom shirt from the 70s. Blue Elkskin, Indian Head Nickels for buttons! CAT

The day of shooting, I didn't want to know what was going on in that limo. Especially because Johnny was in it. —vic

That dog knows exactly what he wants — Emile

SUPER—
FLY

WATO-O-PUNK

Nikki and I were punk rock that night, a regular pair of SID and Nancy. Her. hair. IS. HOT! The dude in back Horacio is hitting a Jay hard. I wore my tattoo out to a party and crazy girls were drooling over me (and German dudes) were trying to buy me drinks... scary. — EMILE

WE JUST DRESSED LIKE THAT. I THINK I HAD ALL THOSE PENDLETONS 'CAUSE THAT'S WHAT MY MOM BOUGHT USED AT THE SALVATION ARMY AND THE WINO SHOES COST A BUCK-FIFTY AT COAST SPORTSWEAR.
— JIM "RED DOG" MUIR

what you lookin at holmes?!
this is O.G. Suicidal tendencies style in Dogtown Surfers gone punk Rock
Fuck yeah
J. Alva

battle of the CLONES

RILEY HARPER

BRADLEE COLEMAN

CRAIG WHITEHEAD

ONE of the little KIDS SAID "Miss, there are 3 twins on this movie."

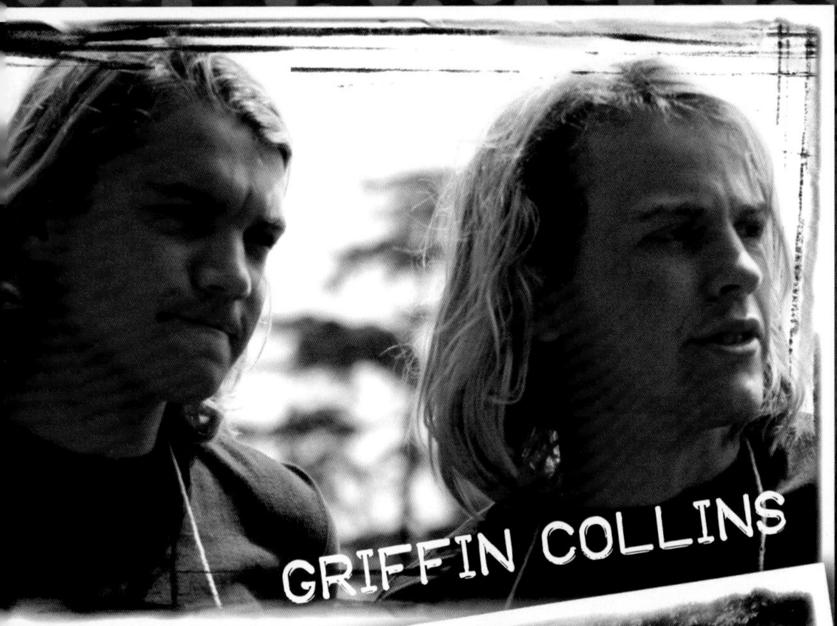

GRIFFIN COLLINS

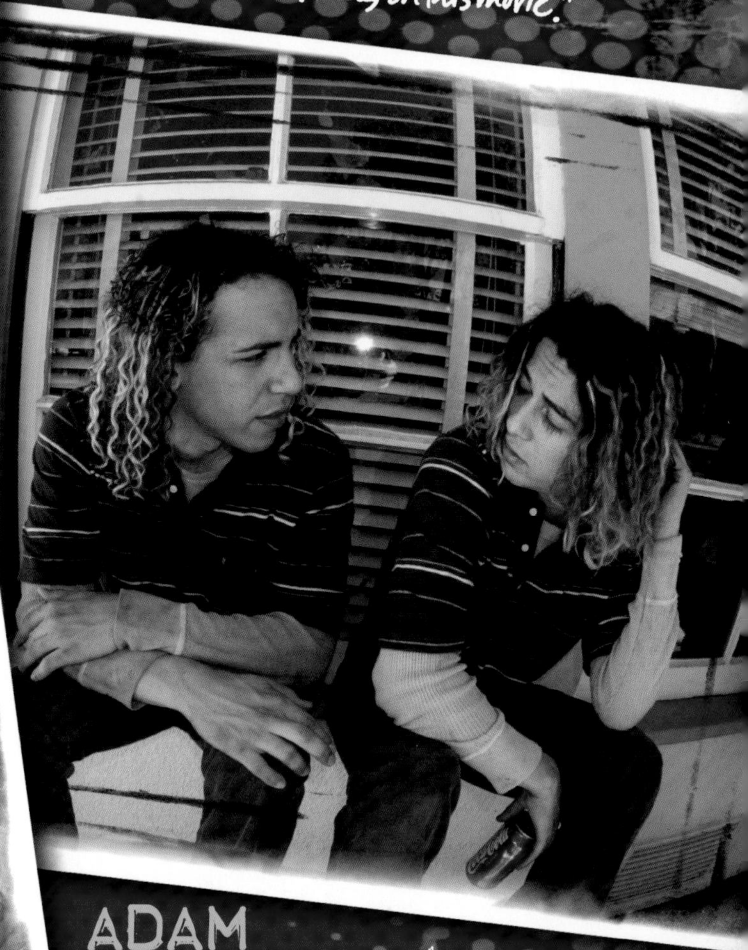

ADAM ALFARO

did these guys Moms shop together P.C.

ZEPHYR COMPETITION TEAM
BAHNE
706
Cadillac Wheels
BAHNE
706
Cadillac

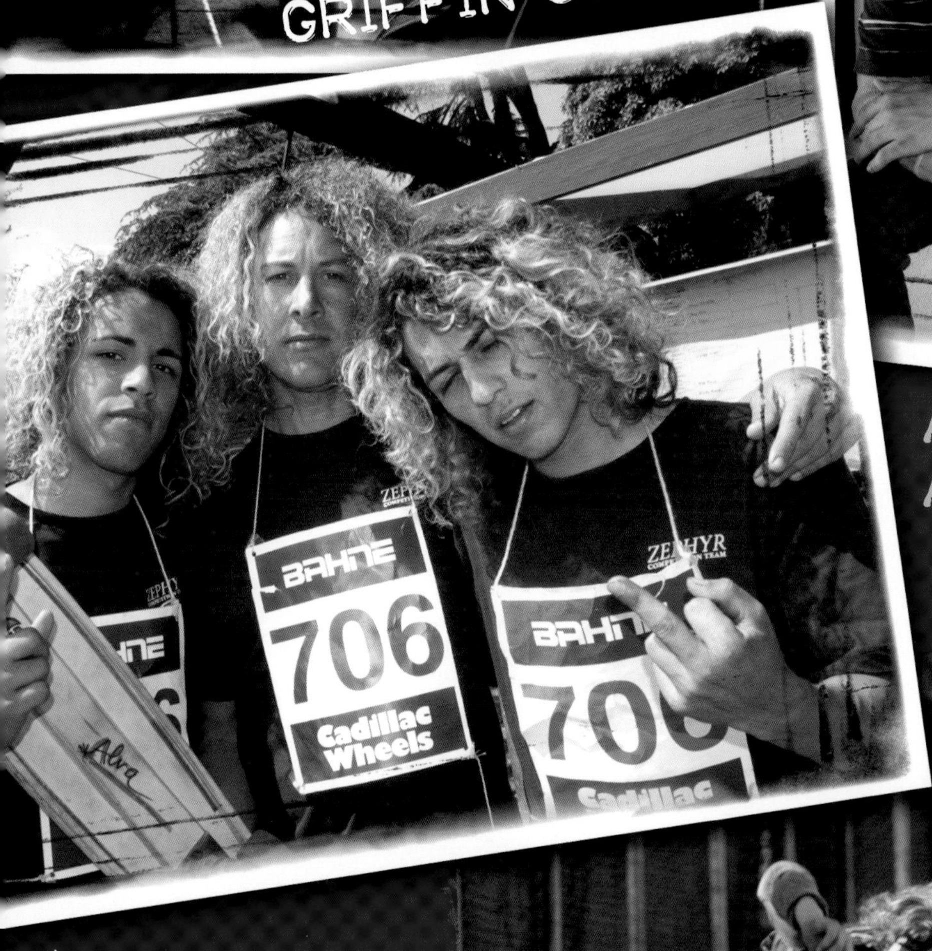

the 3 nappy heads P.C.

PAUL CONSTANTINEAU

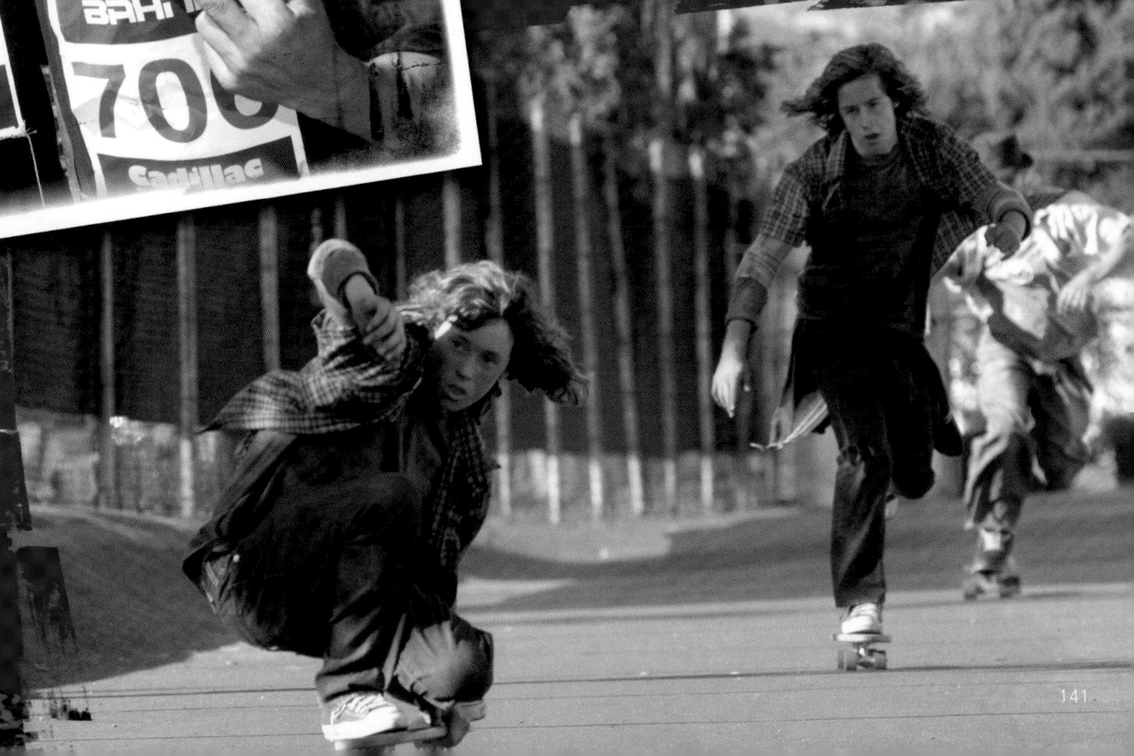

IN CASE WE NEEDED TO DO FACE REPLACEMENT SHOTS, WE HAD TO PAINT DOTS ON THE STUNT DOUBLES' FACES SO THE COMPUTER WOULD HAVE TRACKING MARKS. ULTIMATELY, WE ONLY DID THIS FOR A COUPLE OF SHOTS BECAUSE THE ACTORS SKATED A LOT AND THE DOUBLES LOOKED SO SIMILAR. —CAT

team
MEASLES

I CANT EXPRESS HOW ECSTATIC WE WERE TO HAVE RED DOTS PAINTED ON OUR FACES. A PICTURE SAYS IT ALL.
GRIFFIN

these shady looking characters are the real heroes of this movie. (Sk8 tough or Die! ★
J. Alva

144

I had to ride on the camera bike to keep up with the skaters.
CAT

NO GRILL WARRIOR WOULD
EVER DO THAT TO ME

this is a
FAMILY
RESTAURANT

OH IT'S COOL, HUH? CUZ YOU'RE

From the film

IS THIS THE BEST

A FAMOUS SKATEBOARDER.

YOU'VE GOT, ALVA?

There is pain involved,
we all fell. Griff broke
his fibula and dislocated
his ankle. I twisted my
back. John sprained his
ankle and had to skate
anyway. Catherine fell
head first into an empty
pool and almost died.
Adam got knocked out.
Shoulders were dislocated
skulls smashed in... but
pools are worth it.
Falling does suck though.
— Emile

NAME COLLINS, GRIFFIN
NEWPORT BEACH, CALIFORNIA 92663
361 HOSPITAL ROAD, SUITE 109
MARK A. NEWMAN, M.D.
DATE OF BIRTH 05/15/1983

WE'RE SCREWED

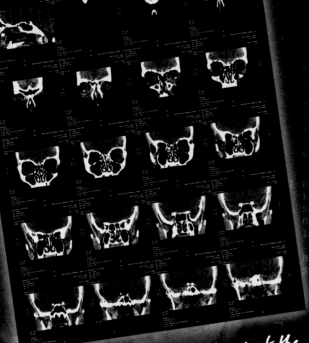

I was directing the boyz at the DOG BOWL — Sunday rehearsal after a looong week. I stepped back and my foot slid off the coping. I fell 13 feet headfirst into the pool. Knocked out and bleeding buckets of blood for nearly 2 minutes. These are my X-RAYS — Do you think I'm OK?

CAT

BRAIN SURGERY

"DON'T WORRY GRIFFIN, YOU'LL HIT THE CRASH PAD," THEY SAID.

~~STRAIGHT UP BRO~~, I MISSED IT!

I CAME TO AT THE BOTTOM OF THE POOL, LYING NEXT TO THE PAD WITH A MASSIVE LUMP ON MY HEAD. BUMMIN'

— GRIFFIN

AND AS THE STUNT CO-ORDINATOR TELLS IT.

I TOLD GRIFFIN TO SKATE TO A MARK ON THE COPING FALL BACK AND THE PAD WILL BE THERE. HE MISSED HIS MARK AND DID SOMETHING DIFFERNT AND LANDED ON THE PAD WITH ITS BODY AND HIS HEAD HIT THE GROUND.

— TOMMY HARPER

Stunt PAD

153

...off the pier

WE HAD KIND OF A PERFECT SUNSET ON OUR LAST DAY OF SHOOTING...

FILM CREDITS

Emile Hirsch
Victor Rasuk
John Robinson
Michael Angarano
Nikki Reed
Rebecca De Mornay
Heath Ledger
Johnny Knoxville
Vincent Laresca
Julio Oscar Mechoso
Sofia Vergara
Pablo Schreiber
Elden Henson
Laura Ramsey
Melonie Diaz
America Ferrera

Casting By	Victoria Thomas
Costume Designer	Cindy Evans
Co-Producer	Ginger Sledge
Executive Producers	Art Linson
	David Fincher
	Joe Drake
Music Supervision by	Liza Richardson
Music by	Mark Mothersbaugh
Editor	Nancy Richardson, A.C.E.
Production Designer	Chris Gorak
Director of Photography	Elliot Davis
Produced by	John Linson
Written by	Stacy Peralta
Directed by	Catherine Hardwicke

CAST

Stacy	John Robinson
Jay	Emile Hirsch
Philaine	Rebecca De Mornay
Donnie	William Mapother
Mr. Alva	Julio Oscar Mechoso
Tony	Victor Rasuk
Kathy Alva	Nikki Reed
Skip	Heath Ledger
Chino	Vincent Laresca
Montoya	Brian Zarate
Stecyk	Pablo Schreiber
Billy Z	Elden Henson
Sid	Michael Angarano
Urethane Wheels Guy	Mitch Hedberg
Browser	Benjamin Nurick
Peggy Oki	Stephanie Limb
Bob Biniak	Mike Ogas
Jim "Red Dog" Muir	Cheyne Magnusson
Shogo	Don Nguyen
Wentzle Ruml	Kristian Peterson
Blanca	Melonie Diaz
Donnie's Friend	Mark Kubr
Mr. Peralta	René Rivera
Reef Ryan	Chad Fernandez
Security Guard	Jim "Red Dog" Muir
Russ Howell	Chris Chaput
Contest Official	Matt Malloy
Del Mar Announcer	Jack Smith
Ty Page	Steve Badillo
Del Mar Judge	Bill Cusack
Bill Bahne	Kirk Ward
Larry Gordon	Eddie Cahill
Gabrielle	Laura Ramsey
Vickie	Sarah Blakely-Cartwright
Restaurant Manager	Bob Biniak
Marty Grimes	Eric Tuma Britton
Irate Husband	Chuck Hosak
Caroline	Chelsea Hobbs
Lookout Boy	Reid Harper
Magazine Reporter	Paulette Ivory
Thunder Monkey	America Ferrera
Amelia	Sofia Vergara
Topper Burks	Johnny Knoxville
Topper's Bodyguard	Raphael Verela
Party Guest	Jay Adams
Peter Darling	Ned Bellamy

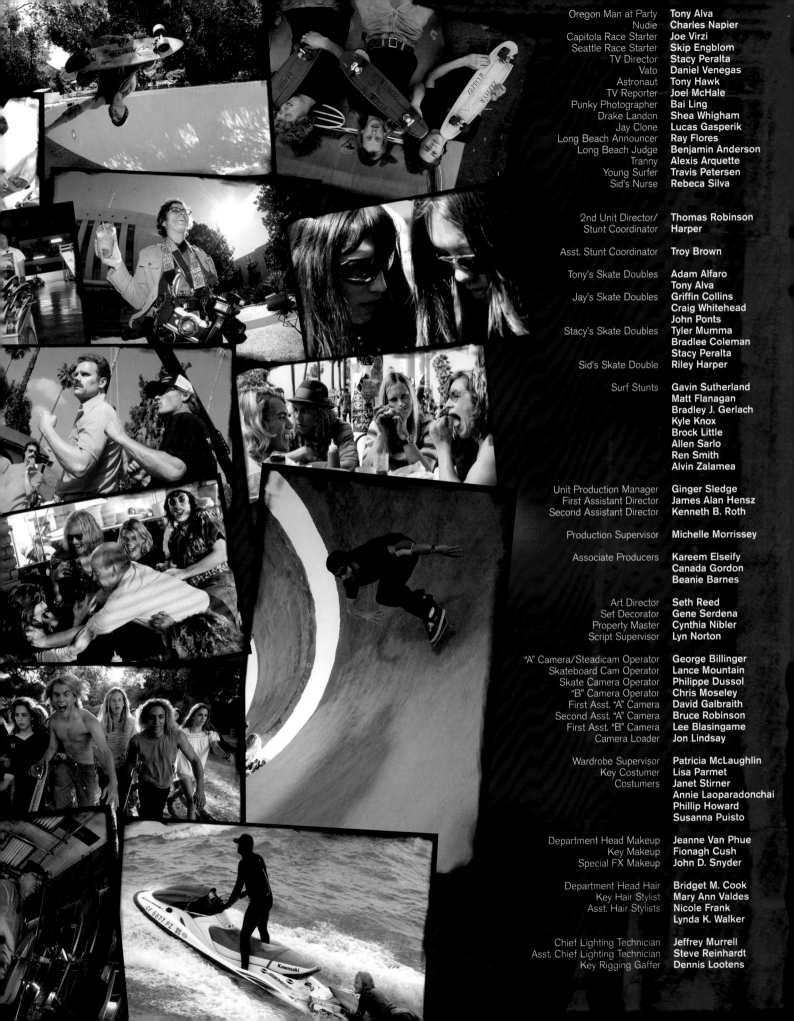

Key Grip — **Richard Mall**
Second Grip — **Thomas Crawford**
Dolly Grip — **David Pearlberg**
Key Rigging Grip — **Blake Pike**

Production Mixer — **Robert Eber**
Boom Operator — **Perry Dodgson**
Cable — **Michael Mesirow**
Video Assist — **Bryce Shields**
Special Effects — **Marty Bresin**

Location Manager — **Bradley Bemis**
Asst. Location Managers — **Greg Campeau**
Ivo Anthony Deranja
David Marmolejo
Production Coordinator — **Diana Zock**
Asst. Production Coordinator — **Vickie M. Hsieh**
Production Secretary — **Michael Steinbach**
Production Accountant — **Benjamin Adams**
Asst. Accountants — **Michael B. Johnson**
Paul Pawlowski

Construction Coordinator — **Lars Petersen**
General Foreman — **Steven C. Voll**
Mill Foreman — **John Sullivan**
Paint Foreman — **Eric Reichardt**
Construction Buyer — **Melinda Frank**
Standby Painter — **Sean Lyons**
Greensperson — **Frank Musitelle**

Set Designer — **Scott Herbertson**
Asst. Art Director — **Gary Warshaw**
Art Director – 2nd Unit — **Maia Javan**
Leadman — **Grant Samson**
Set Dressers — **Mike Boudreau**
Thomas Spencer
Robert L. Stover
Asst. Property Masters — **Tim Mallory**
Robert Smith
Surfboards made by — **Skip Engblom**
Scott Anderson

Unit Publicist — **Linda Brown-Salomone**
Still Photographer — **Jaimie Trueblood**
2nd Second Asst. Director — **Jay Ostrowski**

Asst. to Art Linson — **Carolyn Miller**
Asst. to Ms. Sledge — **Rebecca Whitesell Lafond**
Production Assts. — **Patrick Bentley**
Zach Hunt
Mark McGrath
Michael McGrath
Antonio Scimone
Brian Spirnak

Casting Associate — **Robyn Owen**
Extras Casting — **Deedee Ricketts**

Caterer	Ken & Art's Motion Picture Catering
Craft Service	David Kasubowski
Consultant	Greg Beato
Skate Coach	Tony Alva
Skateboard Trainer	Steve Badillo
Skateboard Consultant	Chris Wessman
Surfing Consultant	Jim "Red Dog" Muir
Animal Trainer	Melinda Eichberg
Transportation Captain	Joel A. Renfro
Transportation Co-Captain	Thomas Lyons

WATER UNIT

Director Of Photography	Don King
Camera Operator	Sonny Miller
Water Safety	Brian L. Keaulana

POST PRODUCTION

1st Asst. Editor	Rolf Fleischmann
Apprentice Editor	Harry Yoon
Sound Supervision & Design	Bruce D. Fortune, M.P.S.E.
	Lance Brown
Asst. Sound Editors	Tricia Linklater
	Mario A. Vitale, M.P.S.E.
	Todd M. Harris
Dialogue Editors	Nancy Kyong Nugent
	John C. Stuver, M.P.S.E.
Sound Effects Editors	Howard S.M. Neiman
	Eddie Kim
	Roland N. Thai M.P.S.E.
ADR Supervisor	Devon Curry M.P.S.E.
Foley Supervisor	Thom Brennan
Foley Editor	Lisa Varetakis
Foley Mixers	Brian Ruberg
	Kyle Rochlin
Foley Artists	Gary Hecker
	Nancy Parker
	Vince Guisetti
	Pamela Nedd Kahn
ADR Mixers	Howard London, C.A.S.
	David Weisberg
	Brian Smith
Re-Recordist	Fred W. Peck III
Supervising Sound Mixers	Bob Beemer
	Tateum Kohut
	Rick Kline
Voice Casting by	The Reel Team
Post Services Provided by	Sony Pictures Studios Culver City, California
Music Editor	Jennifer Nash
Score Mixers	Van Coppock
	Bob Casale
Music Consultants	Bob Badami
	Kelly Curtis
Main Titles by	Kaleidoscope Films Group
Opticals by	Pacific Title
Digital Intermediate by	FotoKem Digital Film Services
Color Timer	Walter Volpatto
Negative Cutter	Mo Henry
Visual Effects Supervisor	Gray Marshall
Visual Effects Producer	Margaux Mackay

Visual Effects by Gray Matter FX

3D Supervisor	Tom Lynnes

Compositors	**Dan Trezise**
	Stuart Cripps
	Joey Brattesani
	Nancy Hyland
	Cesar Romero
Matte Painter	**Bob Scifo**
3D Match Mover	**Messrob Torikian**
Roto Artist	**Jackie Allard**
Paint/Roto Artist	**Amanda Finkelberg**
CG Artist	**Beau Cameron**
Digital Effects Producer	**Di Giorgiutti**
Digital Effects Coordinator	**Christopher Almerico**
I/O	**Billy Barnhart**
Assistant Coordinator	**Jennifer Mizener**
Controller/Accountant	**Anzhey Barantsevich**
Systems Administrator	**Eric Jordan**

Soundtrack on Geffen Records

Additional footage provided by:

Ira Opper Films
Hal Jepsen Films
KABC-TVUCLA Film and Television Archive
Action Sports – Scott Dittrich Films – All Stock
Ray Allen

"The Sonny & Cher Comedy Hour" footage
courtesy of Paul Brownstein Productions
Archival Playboy Magazine material ©1974 by Playboy.
The Bunny Costume is a trademark of
Playboy Enterprises International, Inc.
Used with permission. All rights reserved.

Vintage Photos and Surfboard Artwork by
C.R. Stecyk III
Vintage Photos by Art Brewer

Rolling Stone Magazine Layout
and Character Portrayal
Courtesy of Rolling Stone
The filmmakers were inspired by
original photographs from the books
"F**K YOU HEROES" and
"DOGTOWN – The Legend of the Z-BOYS"

Special Thanks to
Philaine Romero
Bill Bahne & Bahne Skateboards
G&S Skateboards, Larry Gordon and Debra Gordon
Body Glove
City of Imperial Beach
BURNING FLAGS PRESS

ACKNOWLEDGEMENTS

Graphic Design by
Mark Tzerelshtein
Will Eliscu

Published by
Michael Brooke
Concrete Wave Editions

Illustrations and storyboards by
Chris Gorak
Chris Buchinsky
Catherine Hardwicke

Working drawings by
Seth Reed
Scott Herbertson
J. Andre Chaintreuil

Additional photos by
Chris Gorak
Cale Wilbanks
Brian Zarate

Various imagery throughout the film and this book inspired by original photographs
published in the Burning Flags Press books:
"FUCK YOU HEROES", "FUCK YOU TOO"
and "**DOGTOWN – The Legend of the Z -BOYS"**
www.BurningFlags.com

BIG THANKS TO:
Gary Warshaw
Beanie Barnes
Harry Yoon
Jennifer Janes
Lindy Smith
Brian Spirnak
Fotokem
John Nicolard
Walter Volpatto
Jim "Red Dog" Muir & Dogtown Skates
LA Times
Sundance Institute
Aurora Belchic
Jonathan Baker